LETTER TO LEO

St. Proterius of Alexandria

Translated by: D.P. Curtin

Dalcassian
Publishing
Company
PHILADELPHIA, PA

LETTER TO LEO

Copyright @ 2009 Dalcassian Publishing Company

All rights reserved. No part of this publication may be reproduced, distributed, or transmitted in any form or by any means, including photocopying, recording, or other electronic or mechanical methods, without the prior written permission of the publisher, except in the case of brief quotations embodied in critical reviews and certain other non-commercial uses permitted by copyright law. For permission request, write to Dalcassian Publishing Company at dalcassianpublishing at gmail.com

ISBN: 979-8-8690-6337-3 (Paperback)

Library of Congress Control Number:
Author: Curtin, D.P. (1985-)

Printed by Ingram Content Group, 1 Ingram Blvd, La Vergne, Tennessee

First printing edition 2009.

LETTER TO LEO

LETTER TO LEO

Greetings in the Lord to my beloved brother and priest Leo Proterius.

Our most pious and most faithful emperor Marcianus has recently written a letter to us, in which he asserted that some people do not consider the day of the paschal festival carefully written down, which is to be celebrated by the eighth indictment to come, in the presence of the Lord. However, he did not say this because he was moved by himself, but because he received the writings of your holiness. And he commanded that we should carefully investigate the case, using a very minute scrutiny, which would contain much concern and study. Wherefore it was not to be neglected, that I should at once promote the business; when from that time already when I received the reminder of your veneration, I had the greatest concern for this matter; now examining the legal books, now touching the institutions of the ancient doctors; from which it is possible to investigate this kind of calculation more skillfully. Taking also the centenary course of the Passover, described by the most blessed Father and our co-bishop Theophilus, and running through it all, find it carefully and completely composed, so that, whoever he may be, he cannot in any way criticize and reproach the authority of this scripture. For it was inconsequential that a man so watchful and dear to God, and rich in the knowledge of the divine Scriptures, should have been able to transgress in so great and necessary a business, by neglecting the labor of diligence. But perhaps, as your holiness writes, it is a mistake of a false code, or of a librarian; and therefore, it would be necessary for us to transfer the day of that holy festival, which is absent. But it should rather be celebrated in such a way that it contains the centennial course of the same of our blessed Father and co-bishop Theophilus; which entirely agrees with the pages of the ancients, that is, on the day of the month Pharmoth, according to the Egyptians, which is the 8th of the month of May And for us, and the whole Egyptian region, and the whole East, we are going to celebrate that very day, in honor of God.

But in order that we may not be determined absolutely to write or wish to confirm what seems to us, we also add to this letter reasons which your holiness may appreciate, that it is not necessary to criticize the truth of the Church of Egypt, which existed as the mother of this kind of work, and carefully wrote it down. Once upon a time, the Lord through Moses signified the paschal time, saying: "Keep the month of the new ones," declaring that this is the first time; as he says again: "This month is the beginning of months for you, it will be the first of the months of the year; and you shall make the Passover to the Lord your God on the 14th day of the first month." But the Lord who spoke these things through Moses, existing in the fullness of the law, when he was deigned to become man, on the fifth of the Sabbaths, the fourteenth moon of the first month, eating the Passover in the upper room with the disciples, is betrayed by Judas a little later: and on the following day, the fifteenth moon, he is crucified, that is it is Friday; and having descended into hell, having completed the dispensations of our salvation, on the evening of the Sabbath, in the light of Sunday, he rose from the dead; on which day the moon of the first month near the Hebrews, it is evident, existed. We Christians, then, do not only require the 14th moon in the Passover (for the Jews doing this, they are without a festival); but we also observe more anxiously the day of our Redeemer's resurrection, which is the 17th moon of the aforementioned first new month. If the full moon always occurred in the same way, on the fifth of the Sabbath, when the Savior ate the Passover with the disciples, all doubt would be removed. But because the circle of the moon is unequal to the course of the sun, and the 14th paschal moon often occurs on a Sunday, it is not possible to celebrate the festival then; but not to break the fast the day before, on Saturday, the 13th of the moon; it must be postponed to the following week; especially when we have within it the 15th month, when, as the Apostle wrote, Christ our Passover was sacrificed. For on the fourteenth of the moon of the first month near the Hebrews, as was said above, Jesus ate the typical Passover; but on the following Friday, the 15th of the moon, as a sheep to be slain, he was nailed to the cross for us; and on the evening of the Sabbath, at dawn on Sunday, the 17th moon, he rose from the dead.

Because therefore in the coming solemnity of the paschal, by the 8th indictment, on the 22nd day of Pharmoth of the new month, which is the 15th cal. In May, the 14th moon occurs on Sunday, and it is agreed to postpone it to the following week. For having within it a three-day mystery, that is, the 15th moon, when Christ was crucified, being connected with the fourteenth; nor the 16th and the following tenth and the seventh; Indeed, on the twenty-eighth day of the month of Pharmoth, which is the 9th of the month. In May, we will break the fast on the evening of the Sabbath. But on the following bright Sunday, the 29th day of the month of Pharmoth itself, which is the 8th of the month. We will celebrate the festival of May very sincerely.

For even in ancient times, if the fourteenth moon was discovered on a Sunday, the festival was extended into the following week. As in the eighty-ninth and ninety-third years of Diocletian's reign he was approved. For our most blessed Fathers are declared to have done so even then (in the year of Christ 373). Indeed, in the eighty-ninth year of the reign of Diocletian, the survivor of our father and bishop Athanasius of blessed memory, with the 14th of the paschal moon on the 28th day of the month of Phamenoth, that is, the ninth month. On the day of April, he had arrived, on Sunday; it was transferred to the following week; so that on the fifth day of the month of Pharmoth, that is, on the first day of the calendar of April, Easter Sunday was celebrated. And in the ninety-third year of the reign of the same Diocletian, when the 14th of the paschal moon, the 14th day of the month of Pharmoth, which is the 5th of April, fell on a Sunday, a postponement was made to the following week: so that Easter Sunday was the 21st day of the month of Pharmoth, which is the

16th of calend . In May, it was celebrated solemnly. In the hundred and third year from the reign of the aforesaid Diocletian (the year of Christ 387), with the fourteenth of the paschal moon on the 23rd day of Pharmoth, which is the 14th calend. In May, it would be on Sunday; again, the week was sought, and Easter Sunday on the day of the month Pharmoth itself, which is the 7th calend. May, it is agreed, was celebrated, because of the impending straightness of the time. Likewise, when in the one hundred and sixtieth year (the year of Christ 444) from the reign of Diocletian, the 14th of the paschal moon of Pharmoth on the 23rd day, which is the 14th calend. It will occur on the third day of the week of May, and we remember that we celebrated Easter Sunday on the 28th day of the month of Pharmoth, which is the ninth day of May.

It is necessary, therefore, in the 250th year of the reign of Diocletian, on the future paschal festival of the eighth indiction, on the twenty-second day of Pharmoth, which is the 15th of the month. The fourteenth moon of May, occurring on a Sunday, was suitably extended into the next week, according to the preceding form, as the 29th day of the month of Pharmoth, which is the 8th calend. In May, let us celebrate Easter on Sunday, because of the griping distress again; as our Fathers did, meeting the fourteenth moon on Sunday, different. For if we celebrate Easter on the 22nd day of the month of Pharmoth, which is the 15th calends of May, the 14th moon, as I said, often occurring on a Sunday, we shall find that the previous day, that is, on the Sabbath, the 21st day of the same month, which is the 16th calends of May, the 13th moon being then not to break the fast properly. Nor is Passover eaten on the thirteenth of the moon. Hence, because on the 22nd day of the month Pharmoth, which is the fifteenth calends of May, on Sunday, the fourteenth moon occurs; but it is not fitting to fast on Sunday, because this is characteristic of the Manichaeans: the consequence is to stretch into the next week, within which, as we have said, we have both the 15th moon, when the Lord was crucified, and the 16th moon, and at the same time the 17th moon, when he rose from the dead. So that is the 28th day of the month of Pharmoth, which is the 9th of the month. May, on the evening of the Sabbath we break the fast according to custom, and on the following Sunday, the 29th day of the month itself, which is the 8th month. In May, we will celebrate the Easter festival.

We must also make known to you that in the future year 265 from the reign of Diocletian, the 14th moon occurs again, on the 18th day of the month of Pharmoth, which is the 14th of the month. May, Easter Sunday, the 28th day of the same month, which is the 7th of the month. In May, God will be celebrated with excellence.

But some, not perhaps ignorant of the exactness of the calculation of the Passover, and led astray by Jewish fables, will consider that we should retire into the second month, if we require the festival so far; I do not know exactly whence they assert this. For the 14th moon of the month occurring on the 22nd day of the month of Pharmoth, which is the 15th of the month of May, how shall we bear the complaint that we celebrate Passover in the second month? For the Jews, not knowing the Lord, also do not know the time of the Passover. Hence, they often withdraw from the first month, and in the twelfth month they decide to celebrate Passover to some extent. But our most blessed fathers, affixing more certainly the nineteen-year cycle, which it is impossible to violate, as a ledge and a foundation, and a rule, established this nineteen-yearly reckoning: not according to the uneducated and foolish actions of the Jews now; not according to the putative and fictitious prudence of foreigners, but according to the grace of the Holy Spirit's institution, in the revolution they noted more carefully the fourteenth of the nineteen-weekly circle, the fourteenth of the paschal moons.

Having finished these things, it is also necessary to pay attention to the fact that those who start the first lunar month from the 25th day of the month Phamenoth, which is the 12th of the month, err too much. April, they determine to be at all: by the fact that then the beginning of the spring season, by those who have been able to discover it, seems to have been fixed with all care, and evidently indeed according to the course of the sun, on the 25th day of the month of Phamenoth, which is the 12th of the month of April is known as the equinox. But it is not necessary from this equinox to fix the beginning of the first month, according to the course of the moon. Otherwise, the sun's circle of the moon should have been in harmony with everything. But since it is certain to all who have understanding that the most rapid motion of the moon does not in any way follow the course of the sun, let us now briefly, by God's grace, instruct the doubtful, that we cannot in any way go beyond the second month. For if at the equinox, that is the 25th day of the month Phamenoth, which is the 12th of the month of April, according to the course of the moon, was established as the beginning of the month, and it would be reasonable for some to think that we could retire into the second month. And now, because the 14th moon of the first month by the eighth indication, which will come on the 22nd day of the month Pharmoth, which is the 15th of the month of May, it is found, is certain that the beginning of the same first month, according to the course of the moon, occurs on the ninth day of Pharmoth, which is the day before the ninth of April. When then, the fourteenth moon is found on the 22nd day of the month of Pharmoth, which is the 15th of May, Easter Sunday is found on the 29th day of the month of Pharmoth, which is the 8th of the month. Celebrating May, let us not at all go back to the second month, and let us then undoubtedly consider it the 21st month. How, then, shall we run into the second month, since the beginning of the first month, according to the course of the moon, as was said a little before, is on the 9th day of the month of Pharmoth, which is not the day before. April exists, and the 14th moon, the 22nd day of the month itself, that is the 15th of the month. Will it come out in May? Now, this has been declared in this way, it is certain that we do not run into the second month, the 29th day of the month of Pharmoth, which is the 8th of the month of May, celebrating Easter Sunday.

Therefore, through your holiness, let those who doubt those parts know that we are legitimately celebrating the Passover through the eighth indictment. For this reason, I wrote, following the Fathers and in this the ecclesiastical formulas, and from there assuming the opportunities of this matter. For in this way also our predecessors, if ever a doubt arose, hastened to foretell that the holy festival should be celebrated everywhere in unison. Even now, according to the ancient custom, we believe that in the Lord one faith, one baptism, and one most sacred paschal solemnity are to be preached in the churches by all Christians everywhere in Christ Jesus our Lord; because in him we live, and move, and have our being.

But to translate this epistle into the speech of the Latin voice, we thought it not quite certain; Lest perhaps they, rather among us, becoming Greek, and no longer being able to express these things carefully, should injure the truth, because of a formless and incongruous speech, and which perhaps cannot be so ardently and knowingly translated, as the case demanded. Salute those that are with thee, in fraternity. He who is with us greets you in the Lord. And with another hand: I beg you, sir, to remember you and ours, my dearest and most desired brother.

LATIN TEXT

Epistola ad Leonem

Domino meo dilectissimo fratri et consacerdoti Leoni Proterius in Domino salutem.

Piissimus et fidelissimus imperator noster Marcianus litteris nuper ad nos venerabilibus usus est, quibus asseruit aestimare quosdam non diligenter ascriptam diem festi paschalis, quae per octavam indictionem futuram, Domino praestante, celebranda est. Verumtamen non velut a se commotus hoc indicavit, sed quia scripta tuae sanctitatis acceperit. Et praecipiebat oportere nos causam diligenter inquirere, adhibita nimis tenuissima scrutatione, quae multum sollicitudinis ac studii contineret. Quapropter negligendum non fuit, quominus statim negotium ventilarem; quando ex illo jam tempore quo commonitorium tuae venerationis accepi, plurimam curam rei hujus habuerim; nunc legales libros inspiciens, nunc antiquorum doctorum instituta contingens ; ex quibus possibile est hujusmodi computum investigare solertius. Sumens etiam et centenalem cursum Paschae, descriptum a beatissimo Patre et coepiscopo nostro Theophilo, omnemque decurrens, ita reperi diligenter integreque compositum, ut, quicunque ille sit, auctoritatem scripturae hujus quolibet modo reprehendere ac vituperare non possit. Erat enim inconsequens virum ita vigilantem Deoque charissimum, divinarum etiam ditatum scientia Scripturarum, in negotio tam magno ac necessario, praetermisso diligentiae labore, potuisse delinquere. Sed forte, sicut tua sanctitas scribit, mendosi codicis, aut librarii error est; et propterea nos oporteret diem sanctae illius festivitatis transferre, quod absit. Celebretur autem ita potius, ut centenarius annorum cursus ejusdem beatissimi Patris nostri et coepiscopi Theophili continet; qui antiquorum paginis omnino concordat, id est, die mensis Pharmothi, juxta Aegyptios, qui est VIII cal. Mai. Et nos enim, et tota Aegyptia regio, atque Oriens universus, sic ipsum diem celebraturi sumus, Deo praestante.

Ut autem non arbitremur absolute, quae nobis videntur, scribere seu velle firmare, inseruimus etiam causas huic epistolae, quibus tua sanctitas forte aestimet, non se debere reprehendere Aegyptiorum Ecclesiae veritatem, quae mater hujusmodi laboris exstitit, diligenterque conscripsit. Olim quidem

Dominus per Moysen tempus paschale significavit, dicens: Custodi mensem novorum, primum hunc esse pronuntians; sicut iterum dicit: Mensis iste vobis initium mensium, primus erit in mensibus anni; et facies pascha Domino Deo tuo XIV die mensis primi. Sed qui haec per Moysen locutus est Dominus, plenitudo legis existens, quando dignatus est homo fieri, quinta sabbatorum, decima quarta luna mensis primi, in coenaculo cum discipulis pascha manducans, paulo post a Juda traditur: et sequenti die, XV luna crucifigitur, id est sexta feria; et ad inferos descendens, ad dispensationes salutis nostrae perficiens, vespere sabbati, lucescente dominico, resurrexit a mortuis; in quo die lunam primi mensis juxta Hebraeos, exstitisse manifestum est. Nos ergo Christiani, non solum XIV lunam in Pascha requirimus (hoc enim Judaei facientes, sine festivitate sunt); sed etiam resurrectionis diem Redemptoris nostri, qui est XVII luna praefati primi mensis novorum, sollicitius observamus. Quod si eodem modo plenilunium semper occurreret, quinta sabbatorum, quando Salvator pascha cum discipulis manducavit, omne tolleretur ambiguum. Quia vero lunae circulus ad solis cursum inaequalis est, et XIV luna paschalis in die dominico saepe contingit, non est autem possibile tunc festum celebrare; sed nec pridie, sabbato, luna XIII jejunium solvere; in septimanam sequentem differendum est; maxime cum habeamus intra eam XV lunam, quando, sicut scripsit Apostolus, pascha nostrum immolatus est Christus. Decima quarta namque luna primi mensis juxta Hebraeos, ut superius dictum est, Jesus pascha typicum manducavit; sequenti vero sexta feria, XV luna, ut ovis occisionis cruci pro nobis affixus est; et vespere sabbati, lucescente dominico, XVII luna, resurrexit a mortuis.

Quia ergo in solemnitate futura paschali, per VIII indictionem, XXII die Pharmothi mensis novorum, qui est XV cal. Maii, occurrit XIV luna die dominico, in septimanam differre convenit subsequentem. Habentes enim intra eam triduanum mysterium, hoc est XV lunam, quando crucifixus est Christus, quartaedecimae cohaerentem; nec non et XVI et sequentem decimam septimam; vigesimo quidem octavo die mensis Pharmothi, qui est IX cal. Maii, jejunia solvemus vespere sabbatorum. Sequenti vero lucescente dominico, XXIX die mensis ipsius Pharmothi, qui est VIII cal. Maii, festivitatem sincerissime celebrabimus.

LETTER TO LEO

Nam et priscis temporibus, si quando die dominico, decima quarta luna reperta est, in sequentem septimanam est dilata festivitas. Sicut in octogesimo nono et nonagesimo tertio anno a Diocletiani probatur imperio. Sic enim et tunc beatissimi Patres nostri fecisse declarantur (Anno Christi 373). In octogesimo nono quidem anno ab imperio Diocletiani, superstite beatae memoriae Patre nostro et episcopo Athanasio, cum XIV luna paschalis XXVIII die mensis Phamenoth, id est, nono calend. Aprilium die, provenisset, die dominico; in subsequentem translatum est hebdomadem; ita ut quinta die mensis Pharmothi, hoc est, pridie calendarum Aprilium, celebraretur Pascha dominicum. In nonagesimo autem tertio anno ab imperio ejusdem Diocletiani, cum XIV luna paschalis XIV die mensis Pharmothi, qui est V idus Aprilis, die dominico contigisset, in sequentem item septimanam dilatio facta est: ita ut dominicum pascha XXI die mensis Pharmothi, qui est XVI calend. Maii, solemniter ageretur. In centesimo quoque tertio anno ab imperio praefati Diocletiani (Anno Christi 387), cum luna paschalis decima quarta Pharmothi XXIII die, qui est XIV calend. Maii, esset die dominico superventura; iterum septimana quaesita est, et dominicum pascha die mensis ipsius Pharmothi, qui est VII calend. Maii, constat esse celebratum, propter angustiam temporis imminentem. Item cum in centesimo sexagesimo anno (Anno Christi 444) a Diocletiani imperio, 14 luna paschalis Pharmothi XXIII die, qui est XIV calend. Maii, occurrerit, tertia feria septimanae, et dominicum Pascha XXVIII die mensis ipsius Pharmothi, qui est nono calendas Maii, nos celebrasse meminimus.

Necesse est igitur, in CCLV anno a Diocletiani imperio, in futuro paschali festo indictionis octavae, vigesimo secundo die Pharmothi, qui est XV calend. Maii luna decima quarta, occurrente die dominico, in proximam septimanam, juxta praecedentem formam, convenienter extendi, ut XXIX die mensis Pharmothi, qui est VIII calend. Maii, dominicum celebremus Pascha, propter apprehendentem rursus angustiam; sicut Patres nostri fecerunt, decimas quartas lunas occurrentes die dominico, differentes. Nam si XXII die mensis Pharmothi, qui est XV calendas Maii, luna XIV, sicut dixi, saepius occurrente dominico die, Pascha celebremus, inveniemus pridie, id est sabbato, XXI die mensis ejusdem, qui est XVI calendas Maii, XIII luna tunc existente, non rite jejunia solvere. Nec enim in decima tertia luna comeditur pascha. Unde quia XXII die mensis Pharmothi, qui est decimo quinto calendas Maii, dominico die, decima quarta luna contingit; non autem convenit die dominico jejunare, quia hoc Manichaeorum est proprium: consequens est in proximam tendere septimanam, intra quam, ut diximus, habemus et XV lunam, quando crucifixus est Dominus, et XVI lunam, simul et XVII lunam, quando resurrexit a mortuis. Ita ut XXVIII die mensis Pharmothi, qui est IX calend. Maii, vespere sabbati jejunia pro more solvamus, et sequenti dominico, XXIX die mensis ipsius, qui est VIII calend. Maii, festum paschale celebremus.

Illud etiam necessario vobis innotescimus, quod in futuro anno CCLXV ab imperio Diocletiani, XIV luna rursus occurrente, XVIII die mensis Pharmothi, qui est XIV calend. Maii, dominicum Pascha XXVIII die mensis ipsius, qui est VII cal. Maii, Deo praestante celebrabitur.

Sed nonnulli subtilitatem paschalis computi forsitan ignorantes, Judaicis seducti fabulis, aestimabunt nos in secundum mensem recedere, si festivitatem eatenus exigamus, nescio prorsus unde hoc asserentes. Nam XIV luna ipsius mensis occurrente XXII die mensis Pharmothi, qui est XV cal. Maii, quomodo querelam sustinebimus, quod in secundo mense Pascha celebremus? Judaei namque ignorantes Dominum, tempus quoque Paschae ignorant. Unde saepius a primo mense recedunt, et in XII mense Pascha celebrare se aliquatenus arbitrantur. Sed beatissimi patres nostri cyclum decemnovennalem certius affigentes, quem violari impossibile est, velut crepidinem ac fundamentum, et regulam, hunc decemnovennalem computum statuerunt: non juxta Judaeorum nunc indoctas atque ineptas actiones; neque secundum exterorum putativam fictamque prudentiam, sed secundum gratiam Spiritus sancti instituti, in revolutione saepe memorati decemnovennalis circuli decimas quartas paschales lunas diligentius adnotarunt.

His itaque confectis, illud etiam oportet attendere, quod errent nimium qui primi mensis initium lunaris cursus a XXV die mensis Phamenoth, qui est XII calend. Aprilis, omnino esse constituunt: eo quod tunc initium verni temporis, ab his qui hoc invenire valuerunt cum omni diligentia praefixum esse videatur, et manifeste quidem secundum cursum solis, XXV die mensis Phamenoth, qui est XII cal. Aprilis, aequinoctium esse cognoscitur. Sed non oportet ab hoc aequinoctio primi mensis exordium, juxta cursum lunae, prorsus affigere.

Alioquin per omnia solis circulo lunae discursus concordare debuerat. Verum quia cunctis habentibus intellectum certum est quod velocissimum lunae motum cursus solis minime consequatur, age jam nunc breviter, Deo praestante, dubios instruamus, quod in secundum mensem nullo modo possimus excedere. Si enim in aequinoctio, id est XXV die mensis Phamenoth, qui est XII cal. Aprilis, juxta cursum lunae, mensis constitueretur initium, rationis esset opinari nonnullos, in secundum mensem nos posse recedere. Nunc autem, quia XIV luna primi mensis per octavam indictionem, quae ventura est XXII die mensis Pharmothi, qui est XV cal. Maii, invenitur, certum est quod initium ejusdem mensis primi juxta lunae cursum nono die Pharmothi, qui est pridie nonas Aprilis occurrat. Cum ergo decima quarta luna, XXII die mensis Pharmothi inveniatur, qui est XV calendas Maii, dominicum pascha XXIX die mensis ipsius Pharmothi, qui est VIII cal. Maii, celebrantes, in secundum mensem minime recedimus, eum lunam tunc XXI indubitate habeamus. Quomodo igitur excurremus in mensem secundum, quandoquidem initium primi mensis juxta lunae cursum, sicut paulo ante dictum est, IX die mensis Pharmothi, qui est pridie non. Aprilis, existat, et XIV luna, XXII die mensis ipsius, id est XV cal. Maii proveniat? Hoc autem ita declarato, certum est quod in secundum mensem nullatenus excurramus, XXIX die mensis Pharmothi, qui est VIII cal. Mai., dominicum pascha celebrantes.

Cognoscant itaque per tuam sanctitatem, qui in illis partibus ambigunt, quod legitime per octavam indictionem Pascha peragimus. Propterea enim scripsi, Patrum et in hoc ecclesiasticas formulas subsequens, et exinde occasiones rei hujus assumens. Sic namque et praecessores nostri, si quando dubietas orta est, praedicere festinabant, ut ubique consonanter ageretur sancta festivitas. Quod etiam nunc juxta priscam consuetudinem credimus in Domino praedicari in ecclesiis unam fidem, unum baptisma, et unam solemnitatem sacratissimam paschalem ab omnibus Christianis ubique celebrari in Christo Jesu Domino nostro; quia in ipso vivimus, et movemur, et sumus.

Transferre vero hanc epistolam in Latinae vocis eloquium, non satis certum esse putavimus; ne forte graecissantes potius apud nos, nec jam valentes haec diligenter exprimere, laederent veritatem, propter informem sermonem atque incongruum, et qui forte non ita possit ardenter scienterque transferri, sicut causa poscebat. Saluta eam, quae tecum est, fraternitatem. Te, quae nobiscum est, salutat in Domino. Et alia manu: Valere te et nostri meminisse, domine, precor, dilectissime et desideratissime frater.

The Scriptorium Project is the work of a small group of lay people of various apostolic churches who are interested in the preservation, transmission, and translation of the works of the early and medieval church. Our efforts are to make the works of the church fathers accessible to anyone who might have an interest in Christian antiquities and the theological, philosophical, and moral writings that have become the bedrock of Western Civilization.

To-date, our releases have pulled from the Greek, Syriac, Georgian, Latin, Celtic, Ethiopian, and Coptic traditions of Christianity, and have been pulled from sundry local traditions and languages.

Nile River Valley Church Series (Coptic, Nubian, Ethiopian):

The Holy Ghost by St. Didymas the Blind (Sept. 2008)
Letter to Leo by St. Proterius of Alexandria (June 2009)
The Paradise of Heraclides by Heraclides of Alexandria (Apr. 2013)
Discourse on Mary Theotokos by St. Cyril of Jerusalem (Sept. 2013)
Nicene Canons in the Old Nubian Language (Jan. 2018)
First Book of Ethiopian Maccabees (Dec 2018)
Life of St. Mary the Egyptian by St. Sophronius of Jerusalem (May 2019)
The Old Nubian Miracle of St. Mena (Jan. 2021)
Two Letters by St. Dionysius of Alexandria (Apr. 2022)
Instructions: Counsel for Novices by St. Ammonas the Hermit (Sept 2022)
Religious Exercise and Quiet by St. Isaiah the Solitary (Oct 2022)
The Vision of Theophilus by St. Cyril of Alexandria (Dec 2022)
Second Book of Ethiopian Maccabees (Aug 2023)

www.ingramcontent.com/pod-product-compliance
Lightning Source LLC
LaVergne TN
LVHW061044070526
838201LV00073B/5170